HELP WITH HOMEWORK
MATHS
ESSENTIALS

HI, MY NAME IS *KITCAT*...

... AND I'M *DIG*.

WE ARE HERE TO HELP YOU THROUGH THESE EXERCISES. START AT THE BEGINNING AND DON'T DO TOO MUCH IN ONE GO.

IT WON'T BE EASY ALL THE TIME. SOME PAGES CAN BE TRICKY, BUT WE'VE GIVEN YOU THE ANSWERS AT THE BACK IN CASE YOU GET REALLY STUCK. NO PEEPING, THOUGH! YOU WILL RECOGNISE A LOT OF THIS FROM THE WORK YOU DO AT SCHOOL. NOW DON'T YOU WISH YOU'D PAID MORE ATTENTION?! *GOOD LUCK!*

Autumn Publishing

Number values

Write these numbers in words.

For example:
321857 = three hundred and twenty-one thousand, eight hundred and fifty-seven

a. 53 _____

b. 653 _____

c. 1653 _____

d. 21653 _____

e. 721653 _____

Write these numbers in numerals.

a. Two thousand, three hundred and four _____

b. Nine thousand, one hundred and eighty _____

c. Eleven thousand, three hundred and seventy-six _____

d. Fifty thousand, six hundred and four _____

e. Two hundred and one thousand, eight hundred and ninety _____

Order these numbers from the smallest to the biggest.

a. 7436, 5345, 4201, 6032 _____

b. 5642, 3386, 1916, 11837 _____

c. 1708, 39726, 7951, 131480 _____

Get it?

To order the digits, start from the left each time.

When you order decimal numbers, it can help if you line them up underneath each other.

For example:

0.60
0.06

0.60 is bigger than 0.06

Order these decimals from the smallest to the biggest.

a.   0.01, 0.90, 0.59, 0.73 _____

b.   0.10, 0.05, 0.21, 0.09 _____

Negative numbers

Complete this number line with negative numbers.

-10   -8 -7   -5 -4   -1 0 1 2 3 4 5 6 7 8 9 10

Order these numbers as they would appear on the number line from left to right.

a.   9, 10, -1, -7, -3, -10 _____

b.   7, -7, 4, -2, -1, 9 _____

c.   5, 0, -1, 1, -8, -4 _____

Stick a reward sticker here!

3

Addition and subtraction

Add the units first, then add the tens, then the hundreds, then the thousands and finally the ten thousands.

Remember to carry digits over to the correct columns.

For example:

	TTh	Th	H	T	U
	3	3	4	5	5
+	1	4	2	3	5
	4	7	6	9	0

5 + 5 = 10 so carry the ten into the tens column.

Add these numbers.

a

	TTh	Th	H	T	U
			5	7	3
+			3	3	5

b

	TTh	Th	H	T	U
			6	7	5
+			2	1	5

c

	TTh	Th	H	T	U
		1	2	4	3
+		1	8	0	7

d

	TTh	Th	H	T	U
		2	4	7	2
+		1	1	5	5

e

	TTh	Th	H	T	U
		6	0	3	4
+		1	2	6	5

f

	TTh	Th	H	T	U
	1	5	1	4	2
+		2	3	6	8

Subtract the units first, then subtract the tens, hundreds, thousands and finally the ten thousands.

If you don't have enough units, exchange a ten for 10 units. If you don't have enough tens, exchange a hundred for 10 tens. If you don't have enough hundreds, exchange a thousand for 10 hundreds. If you don't have enough thousands, exchange a ten thousand for 10 thousands.

For example:

TTh	Th	H	T	U
^{1}2	^{10}7	^{13}4	^{12}3	^{1}3
−		6	8	9	4
1	4	5	3	9

Subtract these numbers.

a

TTh	Th	H	T	U
		6	4	3
−		3	5	4

b

TTh	Th	H	T	U
		6	7	2
−		2	2	4

c

TTh	Th	H	T	U
	1	2	9	0
−		7	2	7

d

TTh	Th	H	T	U
	2	2	8	9
−	1	1	9	5

e

TTh	Th	H	T	U
1	3	7	7	7
−	1	2	7	5

f

TTh	Th	H	T	U
2	4	9	3	5
− 1	2	7	0	6

Get it?

Start from the right each time. You can exchange from the columns to the left.

1 ten = 10 units

1 hundred = 10 tens

1 thousand = 10 hundreds

Shapes

Learn the names of these 2-dimensional (2-D) shapes.

Can you draw lines of symmetry on each shape to create mirror images? Which shape doesn't have a line of symmetry?

Parallelogram – opposite sides are equal and parallel

Trapezium – 2 sides are parallel

Square – 4 sides are equal, 4 right angles

Rectangle – opposite sides are equal, 4 right angles

Regular pentagon – 5 equal sides, 5 equal angles

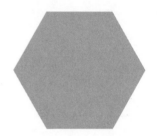

Regular hexagon – 6 equal sides, 6 equal angles

Rhombus – 4 equal sides, opposite sides are parallel

Kite – adjacent sides are equal, no sides are parallel

A **QUADRILATERAL** IS A SHAPE THAT HAS FOUR STRAIGHT SIDES.

Answer: True (T) or False (F) below.

1. A square has 4 equal sides and 4 right angles. ☐

2. A rectangle has equal opposite sides. ☐

3. A square is a quadrilateral. ☐

4. A trapezium has 1 line of symmetry. ☐

5. A rectangle has 4 lines of symmetry. ☐

Learn the names of these 3-dimensional (3-D) shapes.

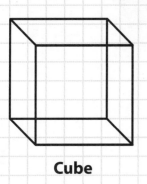

Cube

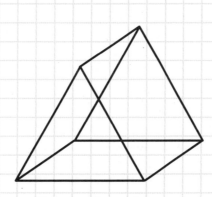

Cuboid

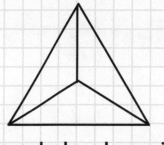

Triangular-based pyramid

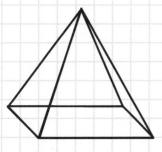

Square-based pyramid

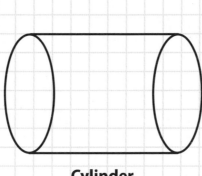

Cylinder

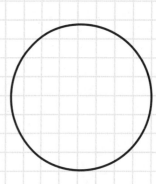

Sphere

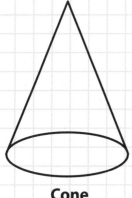

Cone

Triangular prism

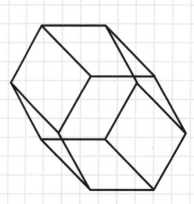

Hexagonal prism

Complete the table below:

Shape	Number of faces	Number of edges	Number of vertices *(corners)*
Cube			
Square-based pyramid			
Triangular prism			
Cylinder			

Multiples and factors

Stick a reward sticker here!

A **multiple** is the number you get when you multiply one number with another number, for example the multiples of 5 are 5, 10, 15, 20, 25, etc.

Count in 3s:

(3)—(6)—( )—(12)—( )—( )—(21)—( )—(27)—( )

Count in 4s:

( )—(8)—( )—( )—(20)—(24)—( )—(32)—( )—(40)

Count in 6s:

(6)—(12)—( )—(24)—( )—(36)—( )—(48)—( )—(60)

Count in 8s:

(8)—(16)—( )—( )—(40)—(48)—( )—( )—(72)—(80)

Underline the numbers that are multiples of 3. Circle the two numbers that are also multiples of 6.

32   36   40   9   30   27   21

Underline the numbers that are multiples of 4. Circle the three numbers that are also multiples of 8.

24   40   80   28   46   15   36

A **factor** is a number that will divide evenly (without a remainder) into another number, for example 3 is a factor of 6, 9 and 12, etc.

Find all the factors of 36:

1 x 36

2 x 18

3 x __

4 x __

6 x __

Find all the factors of 24:

1 x 24

2 x __

3 x __

4 x __

A **prime number** is only divisible by 1 and itself, for example 3 is a prime number.

Which of these are prime numbers? Circle them.

11   15   5   13   7   10   9   12

Work out what the missing numbers are.

For example:

6

3   2

49

7   ○

30

15   ○

28

4   ○

35

5   ○

15

4

12

9

3

16

7

Get it?

even x even = even

odd x odd = odd

odd x even = even

9

Division and multiplication

Stick a reward sticker here!

Complete the multiplication grid.

The first answer is done to get you started.

X	7	5	6	2
3	21			
6				
8				
4				

Multiplication and division are **opposites**.

For example:
8 x 5 = 40, so 40 ÷ 8 = 5 and 40 ÷ 5 = 8

Get it?

When we multiply by a positive number, the answer will be a greater number. When we divide by a positive number the answer will be a smaller number.

Write two divisions to match each multiplication.

5 x 6 = 30

30 ÷ 6 = 5

30 ÷ ___ = ___

5 x 11 = 55

55 ÷ ___ = ___

55 ÷ ___ = ___

7 x 4 = 28

28 ÷ ___ = ___

28 ÷ ___ = ___

8 x 6 = 48

48 ÷ ___ = ___

48 ÷ ___ = ___

Division is like **reverse multiplication**.

For example:

55 ÷ 11 = 5 because 5 x 11 = 55.
You can think of this as 5 groups of 11.

Work out these divisions.

30 ÷ 5 = ___

___ + ___ + ___ + ___ + ___ + ___ = 30

70 ÷ 10 = ___

___ + ___ + ___ + ___ + ___ + ___ + ___ = 70

56 ÷ 7 = ___

___ + ___ + ___ + ___ + ___ + ___ + ___ + ___ = 56

You can work out divisions using reverse multiplication on a number line.

For example:

12 ÷ 3 = _4_

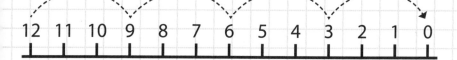

| 12 | 11 | 10 | 9 | 8 | 7 | 6 | 5 | 4 | 3 | 2 | 1 | 0 |

Try it for yourself.

20 ÷ 5 = ___

| 20 | 19 | 18 | 17 | 16 | 15 | 14 | 13 | 12 | 11 | 10 | 9 | 8 | 7 | 6 | 5 | 4 | 3 | 2 | 1 | 0 |

15 ÷ 3 = ___

| 15 | 14 | 13 | 12 | 11 | 10 | 9 | 8 | 7 | 6 | 5 | 4 | 3 | 2 | 1 | 0 |

Perimeter and area

The **perimeter** is the total distance around the edges (sides) of a shape.

Measure these shapes to find the perimeter.

a
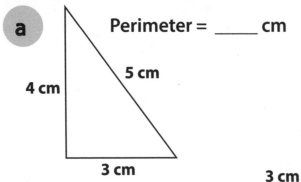
Perimeter = _____ cm

5 cm
4 cm
3 cm

b
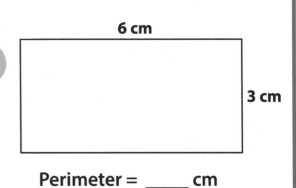
6 cm
3 cm
Perimeter = _____ cm

c
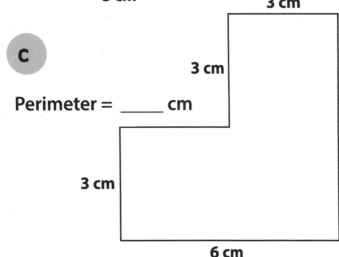
Perimeter = _____ cm

3 cm
3 cm
3 cm
6 cm

d
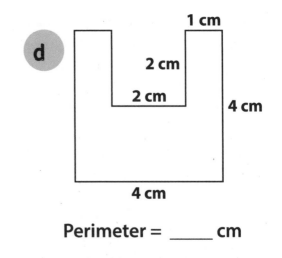
1 cm
2 cm
2 cm
4 cm
4 cm
Perimeter = _____ cm

Measure these shapes and find the perimeter.

a
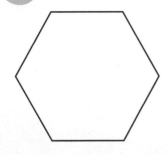
Perimeter = _____ cm

b
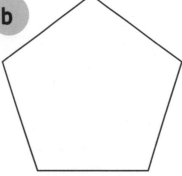
Perimeter = _____ cm

c
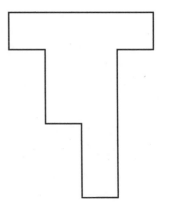
Perimeter = _____ cm

The **area** is the measurement of the space inside the shape.
To find the area of a square or rectangle, you multiply the length
by the width.

For example:
This rectangle has an area of 8 cm².

4 cm

2 cm

Get it?

Area = length x width

So, 4 x 2 = 8 cm².

Find the area of these shapes.

You might have to divide complex shapes into rectangles to work out the area.
These shapes are not to scale.

a Area = _____ cm²

15 cm

5 cm

b Area = _____ cm²

8 cm

20 cm

c Area = _____ cm²

5 cm

5 cm

5 cm

5 cm

10 cm

d Area = _____ cm²

8 cm

4 cm

4 cm

2 cm

2 cm

QUESTION:
HOW DO YOU FIND THE
AREA OF THIS TRIANGLE?

2 cm

3 cm

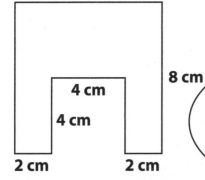

ANSWER:
FIND THE AREA OF
THE RECTANGLE
AND THEN HALVE
YOUR ANSWER.
EASY!

Fractions and percentages

$\frac{1}{4}$ means 1 part out of 4 equal parts.

$\frac{3}{4}$ means 3 parts out of 4 equal parts.

What fraction of these shapes is shaded?

a

b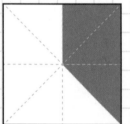

c

You can **simplify** fractions if you can divide the top number and the bottom number by the same factor.

For example:

$\frac{2}{6} = \frac{1}{3}$

Divide the numerator $\quad 2 \div 2 = 1$

Divide the denominator $\quad 6 \div 2 = 3$

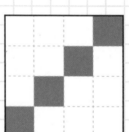

THE TOP NUMBER IS CALLED THE **NUMERATOR**. THE BOTTOM NUMBER IS CALLED THE **DENOMINATOR**.

Simplify these fractions:

a. $\frac{4}{10} = ---$ **b.** $\frac{3}{6} = ---$ **c.** $\frac{8}{16} = ---$ **d.** $\frac{4}{16} = ---$

e. $\frac{5}{10} = ---$ **f.** $\frac{2}{10} = ---$ **g.** $\frac{3}{12} = ---$ **h.** $\frac{4}{12} = ---$

Get it?

$\frac{6}{6}$ is one whole. $\quad \frac{10}{10}$ is one whole. $\quad \frac{12}{12}$ is one whole.

A **percentage** is a part of a hundred.

Learn these fraction and percentage equivalents.

10% or $\frac{1}{10}$									
20% or $\frac{1}{5}$									
25% or $\frac{1}{4}$									
50% or $\frac{1}{2}$									
100% or 1 whole									

Work out the answers.

a. $\frac{1}{2}$ of 50 = ____

b. 50% of 30 = ____

c. $\frac{1}{4}$ of 4 = ____

d. 25% of 8 = ____

e. $\frac{1}{5}$ of £2.50 = ____p

f. 20% of £5 = £____

g. $\frac{2}{5}$ of 25p = ____p

h. 40% of 30p = ____p

i. 10% of £4 = ____p

j. $\frac{1}{10}$ of £8 = ____p

Get it?

1% is 1/100

10% is 10/100

20% is 20/100

Fractions

Colour $\frac{1}{4}$ of this circle red.

Colour $\frac{1}{2}$ of this circle blue.

What is the total fraction coloured?

Which is bigger?

A slice that is $\frac{2}{3}$ or $\frac{3}{4}$ of this pizza?

Colour the pizza to work it out.

Which is bigger?

a. $\frac{5}{8}$ or $\frac{1}{4}$? _____

b. $\frac{3}{8}$ or $\frac{3}{4}$? _____

c. $\frac{4}{12}$ or $\frac{4}{6}$? _____

d. $\frac{5}{12}$ or $\frac{2}{3}$? _____

e. $\frac{4}{6}$ or $\frac{1}{3}$? _____

DRAW FRACTION PIZZAS TO HELP YOU!

Get it?

A **fraction** is an equal part of a whole.

wow!

cool!

fab!

sweet!

wicked!

easy peasy!

nice one!

yes!!

woo!

win!

wow!

yay!

brill!

epic!

score!

woo!

yay!

wicked!

ok!

well done!

yippee!

good stuff!

great!

wicked!

cool!

ok!

brill!

fab!

cool!

ok!

brill!

fab!

yippee!

good stuff!

great!

wicked!

yay!

epic!

ok!

well done!

wow!

sweet!

fab!

woo!

cool!

easy peasy!

nice one!

yes!

woo!

win!

wow!

yay!

brill!

cool!

score!

woo!

Write these fractions in the correct place on the number line below.

Get it?
$\frac{5}{10}$ and $\frac{1}{2}$ are **equivalent** fractions! They mean the same.

0 | | | | | | | | | | | 1

$\frac{1}{2}$ $\frac{1}{5}$ $\frac{10}{10}$ $\frac{1}{10}$ $\frac{7}{10}$ $\frac{2}{5}$ $\frac{3}{10}$ $\frac{4}{5}$ $\frac{5}{10}$

Which two fractions have the same value?

Join the equivalent fractions with a line.

$\frac{2}{3}$ $\frac{2}{4}$ $\frac{3}{12}$ $\frac{3}{9}$

$\frac{4}{6}$ $\frac{1}{4}$ $\frac{1}{3}$ $\frac{1}{2}$

Order these fractions from the smallest to the biggest.

$\frac{1}{2}$ $\frac{1}{4}$ $\frac{3}{4}$ $\frac{4}{10}$

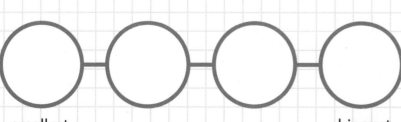

smallest fraction   biggest fraction

WHAT DID ONE FRACTION SAY TO THE OTHER FRACTION? "YOU DON'T KNOW THE HALF OF IT!"

Angles and triangles

An **angle** is a rotation around a point.
We can measure an angle using a protractor.

There are four types of angles.

Right angle:
a quarter turn (90°)

Acute angle:
less than a quarter turn
(less than 90°)

Reflex angle:
more than half a turn
(more than 180° but less
than 360°)

Obtuse angle:
between a quarter and
a half turn (more than 90°
but less than 180°)

* A complete rotation around a point is 360°.

**There are different types
of triangle.**

Isosceles: 2 equal sides
and 2 equal angles

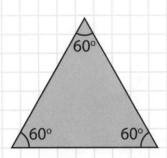

Scalene: no equal sides
and no equal angles.

Equilateral: 3 equal sides
and 3 equal angles

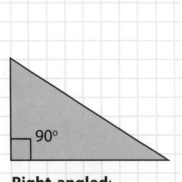

Right-angled:
one right angle

If you add up the angles in a triangle you always get 180°.

Get it?
If you are given two angles, say 70° and 80°, you add these together and subtract them from 180 to find the missing angle.
E.g. 180-150 = 30°.

Work out the missing angles in these triangles.

Label these angles: acute, right angle, obtuse or reflex.

a. 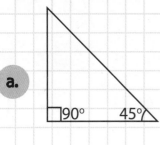 _____

a. _____

b. 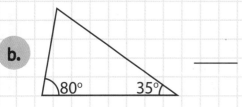 _____

b. _____

c. _____

c. 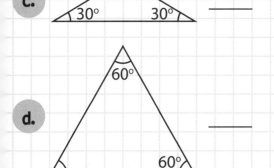 _____

d.  _____

d. _____

Find the missing angles below.
Remember, they should add up to 360°.

a. 45° _____

c. 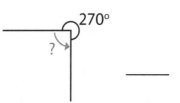 90° ? _____

b.  180° ? _____

d. 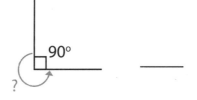 270° ? _____

Coordinates

Coordinates are the numbers we use to mark a point on a graph or map.

When reading coordinates, remember to 'go along the corridor and up (or down) the stairs'.

Plot these positions on the graph.

a. (-2, 2) **b.** (-4, 4) **c.** (2, 2) **d.** (4, 4)

e. (-2, -2) **f.** (-4, -4) **g.** (2, -2) **h.** (4, -4)

Get it?

Another way to remember how to read coordinates: x comes before y in the alphabet, so read the x axis first then the y axis.

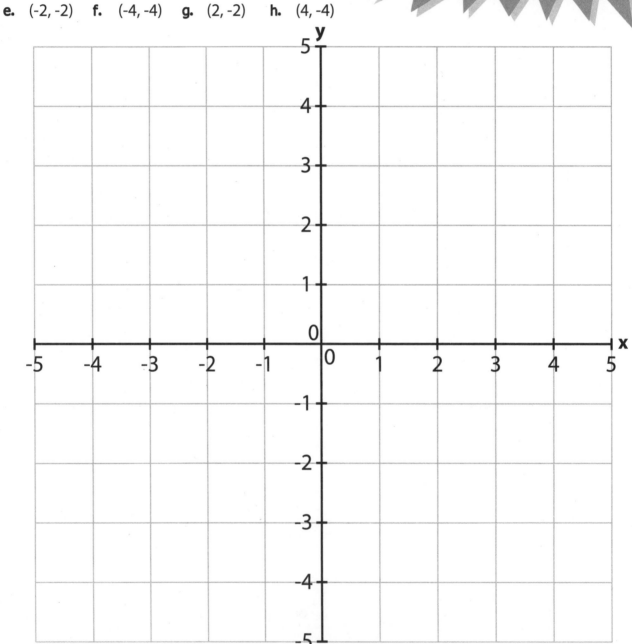

Write the coordinates of the buried bone, which is marked with an x:
(_____ , _____)

Draw another bone on the map and write its coordinates here: (_____ , _____)

Plot these coordinates to find a hidden shape.

(-4, -4) (-4, 2) (-2, 4) (-2, -2)

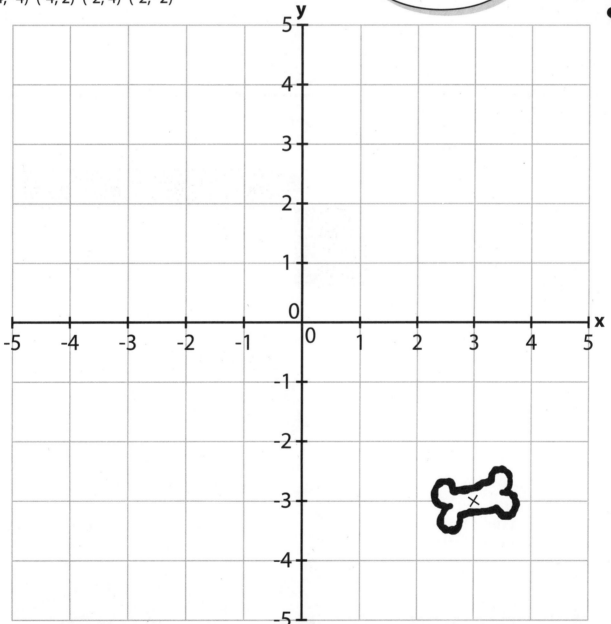

NOW WHERE DID I PUT THAT BONE?

Long multiplication

Here are two methods of doing long multiplication.

For example:

```
    H  T  U
    2  4  2
 x     1  3
 ─────────────
 2  4  2  0   (x10)
    7  2  6   (x3)
 ─────────────
 3  1  4  6
```

Grid method:

X	200	40	2	Total
10	2000	400	20	= 2420
3	600	120	6	= 726

=3146

Find the answer to this multiplication using both methods.

```
    H  T  U
    3  1  8
 x     2  5
 ─────────────
              (x20)

              (x5)
 ─────────────
```

X	300	10	8	Total
20				=
5				=
				=

BOTH METHODS SHOULD HAVE GIVEN YOU THE SAME ANSWER. WHICH DID YOU FIND THE EASIEST?

Find the answers to these multiplications using both methods.

```
H  T  U
3  2  6
x  1  2
_____
           (x10)

           (x2)
_____
```

X	300	20	6	Total
10				=
2				=
				=

```
H  T  U
4  0  4
x  1  6
_____
           (x10)

           (x6)
_____
```

X	400	0	4	Total
10				=
6				=
				=

```
H  T  U
2  1  3
x  2  4
_____
           (x20)

           (x4)
_____
```

X	200	10	3	Total
20				=
4				=
				=

Stick a
reward
sticker
here!

23

Long division

When you divide one number by another number, e.g. 28 divided by 7, it is like finding out how many 7s there are in 28. The answer is 4 because 4 x 7 = 28.

Look at this example:

$$7\overline{)287}$$

We know that 28 ÷ 7 = 4   so   280 ÷ 7 = 40

Then 7 ÷ 7 = 1

The answer = 41

We can write it down like this:

```
        4   1
  7 | 2  8  7
    - 2  8  0
            7
```

Now look at this example:

```
          5  0   r 2
  15 | 7  5  2        r = remainder
     - 7  5  0
              2
```

Try these divisions for practice.

Get it?

75 ÷ 15 = 5   so   750 ÷ 15 = 50.

a.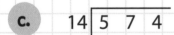
```
20 | 4  8  0
```

b.
```
22 | 6  6  7
```

c.
```
14 | 5  7  4
```

d.
```
50 | 2  6  0
```

Always try to estimate your answers first.

For example:

Share £2.04 between 4 children.

You know that £2 ÷ 4 = 50p so you can estimate that
£2.04 ÷ 4 will be a little bit more than 50p.

Now do the division to find out the answer ...

```
        5  1
  4 | 2  0  4
  -   2  0  0
              4
```

Answer: £2.04 ÷ 4 = 51p

Work out these division problems.

Estimate your answers first.

1. Share £5.25 by 5 children.

2. Divide 568 by 8.

3. 901 ÷ 4

4. If Alice can run 5 kilometres per day, how long would it take her to run 125 kilometres?

5. If Dig eats 156 bones per year, how many bones does he eat per week?

6. If Kit sleeps 147 hours per week, how many hours does she sleep per day?

Do your working out here...

Now try dividing some longer numbers! Practise in the space below.

For example:

```
        2  4  1
 12 | 2  8  9  2    28 divided by 12 = 2 r 4
   -  2  4
         4  9          49 divided by 12 = 4 r 1
   -     4  8
               1  2    12 divided by 12 = 1
```

Stick a reward sticker here!

Decimals

A **decimal** is part of a whole number. It is similar to a fraction.

The number before the decimal point is a whole number. The number after the decimal point is a part of a whole number.

Read the decimals on the number line below.

These are tenths of a whole number.

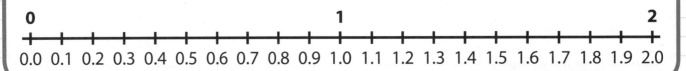

```
0                                    1                                    2
+--+--+--+--+--+--+--+--+--+--+--+--+--+--+--+--+--+--+--+--+
0.0 0.1 0.2 0.3 0.4 0.5 0.6 0.7 0.8 0.9 1.0 1.1 1.2 1.3 1.4 1.5 1.6 1.7 1.8 1.9 2.0
```

Circle the decimal that is bigger in each pair.

a. 0.2 or 2.0

b. 1.2 or 2.1

c. 2.4 or 2.9

d. 3.6 or 0.6

Get it?

$0.1 = \frac{1}{10}$

$0.2 = \frac{2}{10}$ (or $\frac{1}{5}$)

$0.3 = \frac{3}{10}$

$0.4 = \frac{4}{10}$ (or $\frac{2}{5}$)

$0.5 = \frac{5}{10}$ (or $\frac{1}{2}$)

Add or subtract these decimals just as you would do with any numbers.

Put the decimal point in your answer.

a
```
    0 . 6
+   0 . 7
_____
```

b
```
    1 . 5
+   1 . 5
_____
```

c
```
    2 . 8
-   1 . 9
_____
```

d
```
    3 . 5 0
-   1 . 7 5
_____
```

We use decimals in money.

For example:

1p can be written as £0.01

5p can be written as £0.05

10p can be written as £0.10

50p can be written as £0.50

£1.50 can be written as £1.50

Multiply and divide these decimals.

For example:

```
£   2 . 5 0
x       6
_____
£ 1 2 . 0 0   (£2 x 6)

£   3 . 0 0   (50p x 6)
_____
£ 1 5 . 0 0
```

```
        3 . 2 0
     _____
4  |  £ 1 2 . 8 0
```

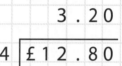

Get it?

Try to estimate your answers first. Make sure you don't forget the decimal point – there is a big difference between £32.40 and £3240!

a. £2.25 x 4

B. £25.05 ÷ 5

C. £16.20 x 2

D. £28.21 ÷ 7

E. Share £14.40 by 6 children

F. 5 lots of 50p

Stick a reward sticker here!

Measures

Learn these equivalents:

1000 grams (g) = 1 kilogram (kg)

1000 millilitres (ml) = 1 litre (l)

1000 metres (m) = 1 kilometre (km)

1000 millimetres (mm) = 1 metre (m)

100 centimetres (cm) = 1 metre (m)

a. Kit can jump 2.5 m. How high is that in centimetres? _____ cm

b. Dig can run 5.4 km without stopping. How far is that in metres? _____ m

c. A quarter of a litre = _____ ml

d. 10 mm = _____ cm

e. Half a kilogram = _____ g

f. 1.50 kg = _____ g

g. 4.9 m = _____ cm

h. 3.2 litres = _____ millilitres

Get it?

2.5 is the same as 2.50

5.4 is the same as 5.40

3.2 is the same as 3.20

a. Which is more: 1000 ml or 1 litre? _____

b. What is 25 kg as grams? _____ g

c. A fish tank holds 20 litres of water.
How many millilitres is that? _____ ml

d. Dig weighs 10 kg. How much is that in grams? _____ g

e. Kit's bowl holds 250 ml of milk. How many
bowls can be filled from 1 litre of milk? _____ bowls

f. Write 1200 g as kilograms. _____ kg

g. Convert 2.5 cm to millimetres. _____ mm

h. Which is longer: 300 mm or 3 cm? _____

CAT-CH!

Multiplying and dividing decimals

When we multiply a decimal number by 10, each digit becomes 10 times bigger and moves **one** place (value) to the **left**. When we multiply by 100, it moves **two** places (values) to the **left**. When we multiply by 1000, it moves **three** places (values) to the **left**.

For example:

4.9 x 10 = 49.00
4.9 x 100 = 490.00
4.9 x 1000 = 4900.00

We can leave out the zeros after the decimal point to simplify the number.

When we divide a decimal number by 10, each digit becomes 10 times smaller and moves **one** place (value) to the **right**).

For example:

$4.9 \div 10 = 0.49$
$4.9 \div 100 = 0.049$
$4.9 \div 1000 = 0.0049$

Get it?
If you run out of digits use zero as a place holder.

WHAT'S THE POINT OF DECIMALS?

I'LL TELL YOU WHAT THE *POINT* IS! WHICH WOULD YOU RATHER HAVE: £10.50 X 10 OR £0.50 X 1000?

Try these:

a. 1.35 x 10 = _____

b. 1.35 x 100 = _____

c. 1.35 x 1000 = _____

d. $1.35 \div 10 =$ _____

e. $1.35 \div 100 =$ _____

f. $1.35 \div 1000 =$ _____

Stick a reward sticker here!

Answers

p. 2-3 Number values
a. fifty-three
b. six hundred and fifty-three
c. one thousand, six hundred and fifty-three
d. twenty-one thousand, six hundred and fifty-three
e. seven hundred and twenty-one thousand, six hundred and fifty-three

a. 2304
b. 9180
c. 11376
d. 50604
e. 201890

a. 4201, 5345, 6032, 7436
b. 1916, 3386, 5642, 11837
c. 1708, 7951, 39726, 131480

a. 0.01, 0.59, 0.73, 0.90
b. 0.05, 0.09, 0.10, 0.21

negative numbers
-10 -9 -8 -7 -6 -5 -4 -3 -2 -1 0 1 2 3 4 5 6 7 8 9 10

a. -10, -7, -3, -1, 9, 10
b. -7, -2, -1, 4, 7, 9
c. -8, -4, -1, 0, 1, 5

p. 4-5 Addition and subtraction

add		subtract	
a.	908	**a.**	289
b.	890	**b.**	448
c.	3050	**c.**	563
d.	3627	**d.**	1094
e.	7299	**e.**	12502
f.	17510	**f.**	12229

p. 6-7 Shapes
symmetry
The parallelogram has no lines of symmetry.

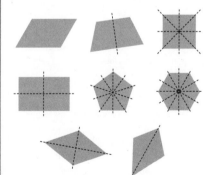

1. True
2. True
3. True
4. True
5. False

Shape	Number of faces	Number of edges	Number of corners *(vertices)*
Cube	6	12	8
Square-based pyramid	5	8	5
Triangular prism	5	9	6
Cylinder	3	2	0

p. 8-9 Multiples and factors
count in 3s: 3, 6, 9, 12, 15, 18, 21, 24, 27, 30
count in 4s: 4, 8, 12, 16, 20, 24, 28, 32, 36, 40
count in 6s: 6, 12, 18, 24, 30, 36, 42, 48, 54, 60
count in 8s: 8, 16, 24, 32, 40, 48, 56, 64, 72, 80

multiples of 3: 36, 9, 30, 27, 21
multiples of 6: 36, 30
multiples of 4: 24, 40, 80, 28, 36
multiples of 8: 24, 40, 80

factors of 36	factors of 24
1 x 36	1 x 24
2 x 18	2 x 12
3 x 12	3 x 8
4 x 9	4 x 6
6 x 6	

prime numbers: 11, 5, 13, 7

missing numbers
3 x 2 = 6
7 x 7 = 49
4 x 7 = 28
15 x 2 = 30
5 x 7 = 35

p. 10-11 Division and multiplication

X	7	5	6	2
3	21	15	18	6
6	42	30	36	12
8	56	40	48	16
4	28	20	24	8

5 x 6 = 30
30 ÷ 6 = 5
30 ÷ 5 = 6

5 x 11 = 55
55 ÷ 11 = 5
55 ÷ 5 = 11

7 x 4 = 28
28 ÷ 4 = 7
28 ÷ 7 = 4

8 x 6 = 48
48 ÷ 6 = 8
48 ÷ 8 = 6

reverse multiplication
30 ÷ 5 = 6
5 + 5 + 5 + 5 + 5 + 5 = 30

70 ÷ 10 = 7
10 + 10 + 10 + 10 + 10 + 10 + 10 = 70

56 ÷ 7 = 8
7 + 7 + 7 + 7 + 7 + 7 + 7 + 7 = 56

reverse multiplication on a number line
20 ÷ 5 = 4   20 → 15 → 10 → 5 → 0
15 ÷ 3 = 5   15 → 12 → 9 → 6 → 3 → 0

p. 12-13 Perimeter and area
a. 4 + 3 + 5 = 12 cm
b. 6 + 6 + 3 + 3 = 18 cm
c. 6 + 6 + 3 + 3 + 3 + 3 = 24 cm
d. 4 + 4 + 4 + 1 + 2 + 2 + 2 + 1 = 20 cm

a. 12 cm
b. 15 cm
c. 18 cm

area

a. $15 \times 5 = 75\ cm^2$

b. $20 \times 8 = 160\ cm^2$

c. $10 \times 5 = 50\ cm^2$
$5 \times 5 = 25\ cm^2$
$50 + 25 = 75\ cm^2$

d. $8 \times 4 = 32\ cm^2$
$2 \times 4 = 8\ cm^2$
$2 \times 4 = 8\ cm^2$
$32 + 8 + 8 = 48\ cm^2$

area of the rectangle: $3 \times 2 = 6\ cm^2$
area of the triangle: $6 \div 2 = 3\ cm^2$

p. 14-15 Fractions and percentages

a. 8 out of 16 parts = $\frac{8}{16}$ (or $\frac{1}{2}$)
b. 4 out of 16 parts = $\frac{4}{16}$ (or $\frac{1}{4}$)
c. 3 out of 8 parts = $\frac{3}{8}$

a. $\frac{4}{10} = \frac{2}{5}$ **b.** $\frac{3}{6} = \frac{1}{2}$ **c.** $\frac{8}{16} = \frac{1}{2}$
d. $\frac{4}{16} = \frac{1}{4}$ **e.** $\frac{5}{10} = \frac{1}{2}$ **f.** $\frac{2}{10} = \frac{1}{5}$
g. $\frac{3}{12} = \frac{1}{4}$ **h.** $\frac{4}{12} = \frac{1}{3}$

a. $\frac{1}{2}$ of 50 = 25 **b.** 50% of 30 = 15
c. $\frac{1}{4}$ of 4 = 1 **d.** 25% of 8 = 2
e. $\frac{1}{5}$ of £2.50 = 50p **f.** 20% of £5 = £1
g. $\frac{2}{5}$ of 25p = 10p **h.** 40% of 30p = 12p
i. 10% of £4 = 40p **j.** $\frac{1}{10}$ of £8 = 80p

p. 16-17 Fractions

$\frac{9}{12}$ (or $\frac{3}{4}$) is coloured
$\frac{3}{4}$ (or $\frac{9}{12}$) is bigger than $\frac{2}{3}$ (or $\frac{8}{12}$)

a. $\frac{5}{8}$ is bigger than $\frac{1}{4}$
b. $\frac{3}{4}$ is bigger than $\frac{3}{8}$
c. $\frac{4}{6}$ is bigger than $\frac{4}{12}$
d. $\frac{2}{3}$ (or $\frac{8}{12}$) is bigger than $\frac{5}{12}$
e. $\frac{4}{6}$ (or $\frac{2}{3}$) is bigger than $\frac{1}{3}$

number line fractions

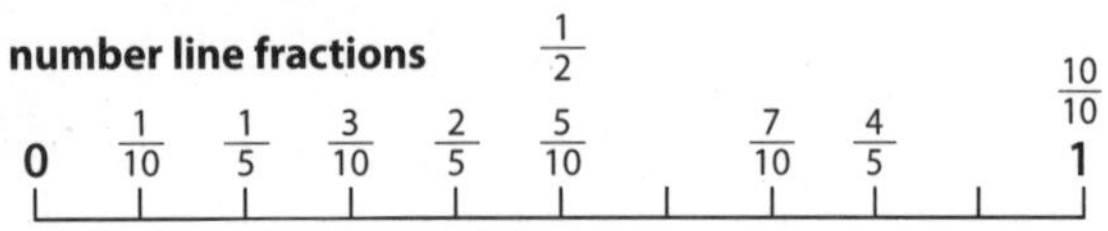

1/2
10/10
0
1/10
1/5
3/10
2/5
5/10
7/10
4/5
1

$\frac{2}{3} = \frac{4}{6}$
$\frac{2}{4} = \frac{1}{2}$
$\frac{3}{12} = \frac{1}{4}$
$\frac{3}{9} = \frac{1}{3}$

smallest to biggest fraction: $\frac{1}{4}$, $\frac{4}{10}$, $\frac{1}{2}$, $\frac{3}{4}$

p. 18-19 Angles and triangles

a. 45° **a.** reflex **a.** 315°
b. 65° **b.** acute **b.** 180°
c. 120° **c.** obtuse **c.** 270°
d. 60° **d.** right angle **d.** 90°

p. 20-21 Coordinates

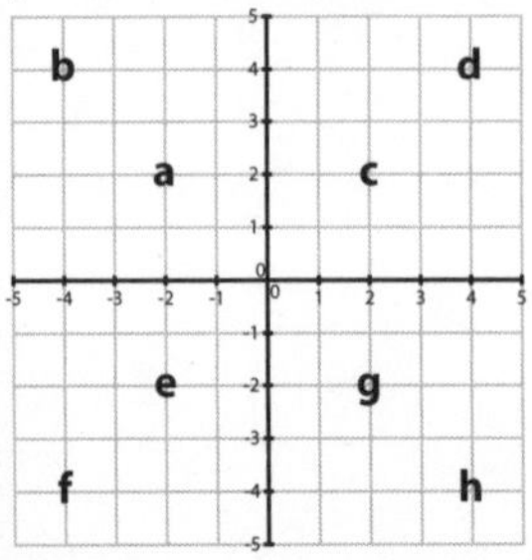

b
d
a
c
e
g
f
h

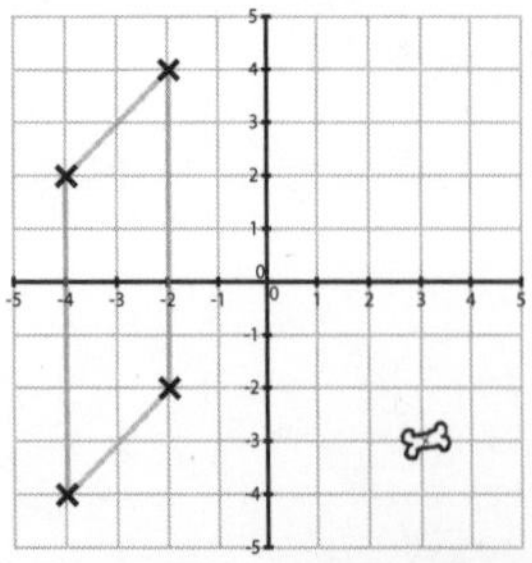

The coordinates for the bone are: (3, -3).
The coordinates (-4, -4) (-4, 2) (-2, 4) (-2, -2) form a parallelogram.

p. 22-23 Long multiplication

H T U
3 1 8
x 2 5
6 3 6 0 *(x20)*
1 5 9 0 *(x5)*
7 9 5 0

X	300	10	8	Total
20	6000	200	160	= 6360
5	1500	50	40	=1590

=7950

H T U
3 2 6
x 1 2
3 2 6 0 *(x10)*
6 5 2 *(x2)*
3 9 1 2

X	300	20	6	Total
10	3000	200	60	= 3260
2	600	40	12	= 652

=3912

H T U
4 0 4
x 1 6
4 0 4 0 *(x10)*
2 4 2 4 *(x6)*
6 4 6 4

X	400	0	4	Total
10	4000	0	40	= 4040
6	2400	0	24	=2424

=6464

H T U
2 1 3
x 2 4
4 2 6 0 *(x20)*
8 5 2 *(x4)*
5 1 1 2

X	200	10	3	Total
20	4000	200	60	= 4260
4	800	40	12	= 852

=5112

p. 24-25 Long division

a. 24
b. 30 r 7
c. 41
d. 5 r 10

1. £1.05 each
2. 71
3. 225 r 1
4. 25 days

5. 3 bones per week
6. 21 hours per day

p. 26-27 Decimals

a. 2.0
b. 2.1
c. 2.9
d. 3.6

a. 1.3
b. 3.0
c. 0.9
d. 1.75

a. £2.25 x 4 = £9.00
b. £25.05 ÷ 5 = £5.01
c. £16.20 x 2 = £32.40
d. £28.21 ÷ 7 = £4.03

e. £14.40 ÷ 6 = £2.40
f. 5 x 50p = £2.50

p. 28-29 Measures

a. 2.5 m = 250 cm
b. 5.4 km = 5400 m
c. 1000 ml ÷ 4 = 250 ml
d. 10 mm = 1 cm
e. 1000 g ÷ 2 = 500 g
f. 1.50 kg = 1500 g
g. 4.9 m = 490 cm
h. 3.2 litres = 3200 millilitres

a. 1000 ml and 1 litre are the same.
b. 25 kg = 25,000 g
c. 20 litres = 20,000 ml
d. 10 kg = 10,000 g
e. 1000 ml ÷ 250 ml = 4 (bowls)
f. 1200 g = 1.2 kg
g. 2.5 cm = 25 mm
h. 300 mm (or 30 cm) is longer than 3 cm

p. 30 Multiplying and dividing decimals

a. 1.35 x 10 = 13.5
b. 1.35 x 100 = 135
c. 1.35 x 1000 = 1350
d. 1.35 ÷ 10 = 0.135
e. 1.35 ÷ 100 = 0.0135
f. 1.35 ÷ 1000 = 0.00135